AlHamdulil'Lahi Rabbi'l alameen.
As Salaamu Aleikum wa Rahmatul'Lahi wa barakatu'Hu.

Praises be to the One, the Lord of the worlds
Peace be to you, and Mercy and Blessings from Him.

January 2006
My pilgrimage: the fifth obligatory pillar in *Islam*

HAJJ JOURNAL

Complex, up close and personal

by Narjis Pierre - hajja'amatul'Lah
photographs by Ali Moshirsadri

Table of Contents

words in *italics* are explained in the A-Z Glossary

Additional copies of this journal
and other peaceCENTER eBOOKS
can be downloaded from
www.salsa.net/peace/ebooks

*The modest amount we charge
for these books
funds the work of
the peaceCENTER*

**Focused on the vision of God's peace, the peaceCENTER
supports the learning of peace in our lives
and the demonstration of peace within our community**

**peaceCENTER
1443 S. St. Mary's
San Antonio, TX 78210
210-224-HOPE
www.salsa.net/peace**

Introduction

Pilgrimage to Mecca or "Hajj" was always an opportunity for me to pause and wonder: 'Why would Allah, Almighty God of Abraham, call Muslims to come from all around the world from every race, culture and language with at least one thing in common, "Islam" to a hot, dry and bare land where Hagar and Ishmael were left at and lived, to perform a ritual which Allah guided Abraham to establish and made obligatory to his nation?

Before I performed my first Hajj in 1997, for two years I was seeking the answer to this question. I studied the Hajj from Quran, Prophet Muhammad and his family traditions; I studied historical and sociological perspectives. All these studies made me more knowledgeable and stronger in understanding the Philosophy of Hajj, but not until I found myself as a drop in the ocean of pilgrimage in Mecca, rotating around the axis of one and only one God, and until Almighty Allah led me to taste the sweetness of his invitation, did I comprehend how deep this ocean could be.

Hajj 2006 was another unique experience, which allowed me to dive in the same ocean, like an amateur diver seeking and learning from this spiritual camp of Allah. Is it not amazing: an ocean in the middle of a desert!?

This time I called my Hajj "Hajj An-Nisa" which means "Pilgrimage of Women". My intention to go on this Hajj, was to perform pilgrimage in place of my deceased mother, who was not able to do her Hajj while still alive.

I was also serving my dear wife Maryam and two of our great sisters, Narjis and Rika. Now you know why I called this Hajj, "Pilgrimage of women".

I like to leave you with a thought: It is said that the Hajj Journey begins from migration of people to Allah, from Allah to people, and to be at the service of people in the way of Allah.

Please pray for me on my continuous Journey and good luck with yours.

Ali Moshirsadri
July 4th, 2007

Rika, Maryam and Narjis at San Antonio Airport

Friday, December 30, 6a.m. at San Antonio, Texas airport

We check in our luggage, and say our good-byes to those close family members who accompanied us to the airport.

Rika and I get an "S" for Special treatment (or security check), and body and purse are searched to start us out on this good adventure.

Somewhere over the ocean in mid-air: trying to nap instead of engaging in social talk as we have done on the previous flights and in our lengthy waits at the Chicago and London airports, where we also meet with other *Muslims* and share in their various connections to this years upcoming *hajj*;

As the talk slows and quiets, the mind becomes occupied with what we are doing and where we are going. Emotions overwhelm and tears stream, joyful and in awe...

"God is really calling us," says Rika sitting in the seat ahead of me. We both seemed to have experienced a moment of reverence, serenity, and indebted gratitude at the same time.

As in the movie we've seen several times, *'Le Grande Voyage' (director: Ishmael Faroukhi; a great movie, highly recommended),* the awareness of time, space and matter as one dimension of reality (the Unseen being another) and being part of the *hajj* experience unfolds as a unique and important process. *Is* it acting as a door to my heart?

A rowdy bunch of women are hovered around the transfer desk in Beirut, Lebanon, arguing some issue with great agitation. We are just waiting our turn at the back of the line, though we do not have *that* much time to get on our connecting flight...but we are *hajjis*, and patience with whatever happens is what we practice. This is also where we for the first time see *Shaykh* Ahmed, who will be our spiritual/*shari'a* "complying coach" for the *hajj* to ensure all rules and regulations are followed.

These ladies, it turns out, will also be our *caravan* companions for the next ten days. Whatever the ruckus was about, we all manage to gather at the terminal; we are given our identifying orange al-Israa (our tour company) scarves, and join other caravans in the airplane. Oh, by the way: at the transfer desk it was one young woman who single-handedly managed to rectify the situation, and with several computers and three men standing idly by, she got all of us on the plane. I loved her for that.

I take my seat in the airplane, and within minutes some man asks if I do not mind switching seats with a friend of his on the other side of the plane. I do not mind, and find myself in the last seat, across the aisle... from the toilet. Well, without much choice now, I put up with the smell throughout that journey, and am greatly rewarded as we approach the city of *Madinah*.

Since I am sitting on the viewing side, as the airplane flies in and circles I am able to see the *Masjid al-Nubuwiyah (Masjid of the Prophet)*! All lit up and huge. The elderly gentlemen sitting at the window next to me doesn't speak any English, and I no Arabic, so there is little conversation, but he understands, as tears stream down my face: I am overcome at the sight and thought of this being *Madinah* and the *Prophets' masjid*. *Subhana'Llah (glory be to Allah)!*

On the plane flying here, *Hajj* Ali's head, a few rows somewhere ahead of me, pops up over the seats and motions to the on-board monitors which show us exactly where the plane is: with his mouth he is saying something (the noise deafens) and I know exactly what it is: 'just imagine: beneath us are the paths that Prophet *Ibrahim a.s.* was taking through the desert country on his way to *Makkah* with *Hajjar* and young son *Ishmael a.s'.)*

Madinah airport is easy, and soon we are together with our luggage on the bus for the short ride to the hotel.

Masjid al-Nubuwiyah

Sunday, January 1st, 2006 in *Madinah al-Munawarra (the city of the Prophet, the Lighted)*

After a short two-hour nap, we get up and are ready to go to the *Masjid al-Nubuwiyah* for *fajr (early morning)* prayer. We actually do not make it inside the building, as the entrance is already filled up with ladies sitting there. We find a place outside among many and settle down. There is a very cold breeze, and the marble floor chills us through, but we are ok. After the prayer, we meet up with Hajj Ali, who takes us on a complete tour around the huge *masjid*.

We stop to pray a *dua (supplication)* on the outside in front of the dome, home and tomb of *Prophet Muhammad (saw – sallalahu aleihi wa sallem – may peace and blessings be unto him),* then turn towards the *Baqi* cemetery and make *dua* for all the inhabitants of the cemetery; then we move closer to the wall in front of *Baqi,* and make *dua* specifically for *Fatima Zahra, Imams Hassan, Mohammad Baqi and Zainul Abideen, may peace and blessings be upon all of them (family members to the Prophet).* Bringing to realization the closeness we now find ourselves to these pure and dignified personalities brings awe and tears. It helps to understand the prayers *Hajj* Ali so graciously translates for us.

Then we're off to breakfast; sleep until its time for *dhur (noon prayer)*, then get ready to return to the *masjid* to be there early to find a space inside for *salaat (prayer.)*

Maryam, Rika and I are blessed to be in the right place at the right time, as after the *salaat* they open up the space for the ladies to visit what is called the *Holy Rawdah*: it is the space between the home/grave and the *mimbar (pulpit)* of the *Prophet Muhammad (saw). Rawdah* is also a name for 'garden'.

Well, the way to this garden is certainly a challenge. I feel like we are cattle at an auction, being herded through channels with *niqab-clad (face veiled)* ladies hanging strapped to the pillars to direct and 'supervise' the extreme and uncomfortable pressures. Many ladies have to turn around and try to make their way back, because they cannot stand the waiting in this suffocating mass of bodies.

Maryam is our lookout since she is the only one tall enough see overhead and guess where we might be herded next and where we should try to push our way to the other side of the pillar. We finally make it, together, to a space, where we (haphazardly) pray two *rakaat (prayer cycles)* assuming we are between the grave of the Prophet and his *mimbar.*

We are being rushed out, as they are closing the pathway channels to prepare the space for the men and *'asr (late afternoon) salaat*.

After the prayer we return to the hotel, where *Shaykh* Ahmed is holding a lecture in the hallway in Arabic on the basics of *hajj*.

Very soon it is time for *maghrib (prayer after sunset)* and we're off again to the *masjid,* rushing in right at the moment of the *'iqaamat (call to prayer*) and amazingly find a nice place to pray. (We are quickly becoming adept at moving among rows and rows of people, sitting, standing or prostrating.)

After *maghrib* we make our way nicely all the way to the front of the women's section, where we stay, pray, read *surah (chapters 55 + 56) Rahman and Waqiah*, and bide our time, comfortably talking with neighbors until *'isha (late night prayer)*. It is very beautiful and contemplative. I have good concentration and focus and am able to make *dua* for our families and friends in San Antonio and around the world.

I pray for closeness amongst individuals (families, friends, among Brothers and Sisters of the *various madhaab – schools of thought)* and for closeness of relationship to *ALLAH SWT.* I do realize that I have to bring my notebook with me in which I have noted down all the the names from my phone list, and where I also keep track of the requested prayers from individuals. My memory alone will never do justice to everyone without the aid of this list.
The *masjid* empties out fast and as we stay longer it is very serene and peaceful. Maryam mentions that we are spending New Year 2006 in the *masjid of the Prophet Muhammed (saw).*

We do not feel like leaving, but we have to sustain our energies: off to dinner at the hotel. We all sit together with a couple that has just arrived from Canada and the chat is lively and happy about Muslim/Islamic issues.

In our room we talk and reflect on the ease with which one could slip into the *ibada' (worship)* of rituals; there is the necessity of a high level of awareness one needs to cultivate not to become distracted by admiration of buildings, objects or persons.

Though we always need to show our reverence and respect for the history of Islam, we may not slip into attributing any powers to any of these historic symbols, and always clearly direct all worship to the One and Only, *ALLAH Subahana wa ta'Ala*. Over the next days we will encounter many times and situations where we witness masses of people, worshippers, where these lines become blurred: are they truly worshipping *ALLAH SWT*, or the historic site/figure?

We finally get some rest and intend to get up at 3 a.m. for *tahhajud* (*superogatory night prayer*) at the *masjid, Insha 'Allah*.

Men awaiting prayer

The gravesite of Hamza (a.s.) at Uhud

Monday, January 2nd

4 a.m.: a wonderful balmy early morning walk to the *masjid* among many other people, all flowing in the same directions, with quiet eagerness to get there. We enter into the *masjid* and find a very comfortable space against one of the pillars, where we pray and make *dua'*. I have brought my notebook, and I pray for the various San Antonio Muslim communities and their leadership, and pray for good helpers and advisers to these leaders; I pray for these communities and people to increase in proper *adaab (courteous behavior)* and for good and effective teachers to all.

Together Maryam, Rika and I read from the *Holy Qur'an*, recite *Asma al-Husna (The Most beautiful Attributes/Names of Allah), dhikr (vocal or silent reflection)* and then stand in line for *fajr salaat*.

We then go outside to join *Hajj* Ali who wants to take us up the pathway to visit *Baqi* cemetery. So many *sahaba (companions)* and *ahlul bayt (people of household) of Prophet* have been buried here. Each one is a great historic figure.

But, first Rika and I have to make a trek to the next restroom: by the end of this trek we have walked a complete circle around the *masjid al-Nubuwiyah*.

This is an anecdote I do not want to forget: once we make it to the toilets, an escalator leads down (sort of into the dungeon). A lady stands at the top and starts talking to me; I guess she is from an eastern European country. I do not understand a word, but am happy about her friendly forthrightness. She holds my arm, and together we step onto the escalator. Only slowly does it dawn on me, that she had been asking for help stepping onto the escalator. Smoothly together we step off, and go about our business. I realize there must be thousands of people who have never in their life seen anything like this contraption, let alone had to actually step onto it!

When we rejoin Maryam, she tells us that *Hajj* Ali is busy trying to get to the cemetery, as, we come to find out, women are barred from the whole area. Many big groups have gathered to pay respect to those who are buried in *Baqi* cemetery. In the meantime, the *Rawdah* area inside the *masjid* is open for women.

Hajj Ali rejoins us. We go to the hotel for breakfast and meet with *Shaykh* Ahmed who inspects our performance of *wudhu' (ablution)* and recitation of *al-Fatiha (chapter 1.)* Rika and I get ready to go back to the *masjid*, while Maryam and *Hajj* Ali stay back to rest.

The ceiling inside the *masjid* has huge sections that are mobile and open up for daylight and close against the night chill. One middle section, in front of the *Rawdah*, has those light sensitive umbrellas. They, too, will open and close at intervals.

After this *dhuhr salaat* we return to the hotel, where I lay down to rest, while Rika goes shopping.

At 3pm our *caravan* is called to get ready for a bus ride to *Uhud*, where the second important battle in Islamic history happened, and also where *Hamza a.s.* lays buried.

There we make *dua*. We climb the hill that played such a crucial role during the battle.

A niqab-clad lady

Niqad-clad ladies all in black (the standard Saudi woman's outfit) are selling their wares laid out on cloth on the ground: I manage to buy a strand of twenty wooden *dhikr beads* without understanding a word of the Arabic, and in addition, not being able to read eyes and face language. Usually I am pretty good at communicating with people of any other language, but now, with the lack of facial expressions and body language, it is very difficult.

We continue on our trip to the *masjid al-Qiblatain. (masjid of the two prayer directions.)* This is the spot, where *Prophet Mohammed (saw)*, having migrated from *Makkah* to *Madinah*, receives revelation to change the prayer direction from facing Jerusalem, as the *Muslims* had done, to now face the *Ka'aba* in *Makkah.* Stucco-decorated arches have small carved decorations of repetitive arrows with two points facing in opposite directions. The women's section is stiflingly small and utterly overcrowded, compared to seeing the vastness of the *masjid* from the outside!

Then there's another visit to a historic site: this time we are at the location of the battle of the Trench, *al-Khandaq*. During *Ottoman* reign, small individual *masaajid* commemorating the location of various figures during this battle were built. There are three left today, all in varying states of disrepair: the *Salman al-Farsi masjid*: small, no doors, just man-size entry arches, adobe, with a bumpy floor covered with prayer rugs.

above:
Salman al-Farsi masjid
below: al-Fath masjid

Time to pray: although space is very limited the two *rakats* upon entering a *masjid* and *maghrib* have not often felt as peaceful and simple as they have here, and that makes me happy. If I'd been by myself, this would be a place to relax into and stay to *dhikr* and worship.

Up steep steps to another small *masjid, al-Fath*: this is where *Prophet Mohammed (saw)* receives the revelation of *surah al-Fath or Nasr: the Victory (110)*. After two *rakaat* for entering the *masjid,* I exit and Rika is there, with *Shaykh* Ahmed, *Hajj* Ali and Maryam. Rika is very upset and cannot understand why these places are allowed to deteriorate and why nothing is done to preserve this historic legacy.

There is another small *masjid*, completely dark and locked down behind bars and walls. This is the *masjid Ali'wa Fatimah*, which is at the location where they found themselves during the Battle of the Trench.

In the back of these three *masaajid*, there is a big, newly constructed, not yet opened *masjid al-Saba (seven-masjid)*-to-be, which will eventually replace all smaller individual ones. This one has the exact same architectural design as all the *masaajid* we visit today (e.g. *Qiblatain and Quba*).

On we travel to yet another historic *masjid*. Wow! What a great site-seeing tour! We continue a short way to the *masjid al-Quba*. Quba is and has been the name of this area.

This is the place, where, after fleeing *Makkah* and hiding in the cave on *Jabal al-Toor, Prophet Muhammad (saw - may peace and blessings be unto him)* and his companion *Abu Bakr (r.a.)* were waiting for *Ali a.s.* to join them. He had stayed behind to fool the would-be-assassins (of *Prophet Muhammed, saw*), and to look after the goods of the *Muslims* who had already left for *Madinah.* While waiting in the area of Quba, *the Prophet (saw)* and *Abu Bakr (r.a.)* laid the foundations for this *masjid*, which is also the first place of worship built in the Islamic area.

It is time for *'isha salaat*: again the women's section is small, even claustrophobic for this many ladies, and filthy. Well, food-filthy, as can happen in our *masaajid* in San Antonio too: small children inside the *masjid* do constitute a very special challenge anywhere.

There is a *hadith (a saying/teaching)* of *Prophet Muhammed (saw)* that says: "Two *rakaat* in the *masjid of Quba* count as if one has done *'umrah"* (a visit to the *Ka'bah* with rituals similar to *Hajj.)*

Reflecting that the *Prophet's* own hands worked in building a first place of worship here really encourages one to study history and NOT to become neglectful and eventually blind, may *ALLAH SWT* forgive us, towards each and every act one can learn from that time in history.

I make *dua'* for individuals in San Antonio who requested specialized prayers, followed by two *rakaat*. We return back to the hotel, very tired, but oh, so full of this wonderful and fulfilling experience.

Dinner is difficult with newcomers at the hotel. Their loudness, boasting arrogance and wastefulness is embarrassing and disturbing. (They are American. . .)

Rika is too exhausted to even think: she falls right to sleep, in her clothes. Though we are tired and are lying down, Maryam and I talk the hours away reflecting on the trip so far and exchanging thoughts about our loved ones at home. I finally just drop asleep, in the middle of her sentence . . .

Masjid al-Nabawi at night

Tuesday, January 3rd

We sleep a few short hours until *iqamat* is called for *fajr*, get up and work our way diligently into the *masjid* as this is late and the masses are already streaming in.

After the prayer, we would have liked to stay to read *Qur'an*, but are disturbed by, and swept up by the movements of the ladies towards the *Rawdah*. We slow down, move close to the house of the *Prophet* and the *ahlul Suffa (people of the bench),* and decide not to enter the squashing again. After salutations to the *Prophet, his family, Abu Bakr and Umar* (whose graves are also next to each other inside the *Rawdah*) peace and blessings be upon all of them, we check out the west side of the *masjid* which is, to our surprise and delight, also a women's section. It has a different feel, is much calmer, 'more mature' . . .

Then we go to the hotel for breakfast.

During the morning we change money ($100.00 = 137.00 riyal) and all together go on a shopping spree: we have been told to do all the shopping in *Madinah*, as *Makkan* merchants don't bargain...

Top: Starbucks is everywhere!
Bottom: Ali, in brown, drinking tea

Hajj Ali is on a search here: he is looking for a 700-year-old compilation that shows the locations of the homes of the *sahaba* around the *masjid al-Haram*.
We return to the hotel to unload, rest and refresh ...but there is no such thing in Rika's vocabulary: she is ready to set out on a second shopping spree. I tag along with Rika, while Maryam and *Hajj* Ali rest some. With our shopping bags we join the *umma' (community)* at the *masjid for dhuhr*, then return to the hotel.

We have some time learning from *Hajj* Ali: he has a map of the cemetery of *Baqi*, and shows us all the people and their relations to the *Holy Prophet Mohammed (saw)* that are buried there. It is very, very interesting.

We have some questions about the surrounding area and the stretch between *Makkah* and *Madinah:* if there are any other historic locations known today that we have seen in the movie*: 'The Message.'* Most locations are known, he says, but not maintained so as not to facilitate the 'pilgrim tourism'.

We take some time to read and study *surah 5:6* about *wudhu and tayamumm (ablution)* as also *Shaykh* Ahmed is checking everyone in the group on their correctness of *wudhu* and the Arabic recitation of *al-Fatiha*.

We return to *masjid al-Nabawi* and stay outside in the front for *Maghrib* and *'Isha*. A picture-perfect beautiful crescent moon is slowly setting between the minarets while we pray for our families and individuals from San Antonio in a balmy comfortable breeze. Sadness sets in as we near the end of our visit here.

We are sitting next to a young Jordanian girl named Lena, and she soon shares with Maryam her own 'Grande Voyage.' Their 17 hour bus ride from Jordan took over 30 hours, because the border guards blocked their bus to check out the credentials of the driver and had dogs sniff through the vehicle after ordering everyone off the bus and out into the very cold at night. Her heart breaks as she shares her distress at seeing the old people from the bus stoically freezing, shivering with no food, drink or shelter. Her mother had advised her to pack plenty of traveling food, so now she was able to share some. Finally making it here, there was another incident at their lodgings, where her husband lost his temper because of some difficulty, and there was an unsettling screaming outburst. Her tears are from the stress of the journey, but also, as she shares: 'she's so happy to be here!'

Masha'Allah. We pray for her to have a magnificent *Hajj* after this trying start, and that all the adventures from now on be better and easier to handle. *Insha'Allah.*

After hugs and feeling like we met a Sister we do not want to leave, we return to the hotel for dinner. *Hajj* Ali has picked up some antibiotics. We all crave the comfort of soup and tea.

We are overdue for some sleep, but as this is the last night in *Madinah*, we all plan to be up again soon and stay at the *masjid* for an extended time. *Insha'Allah.*

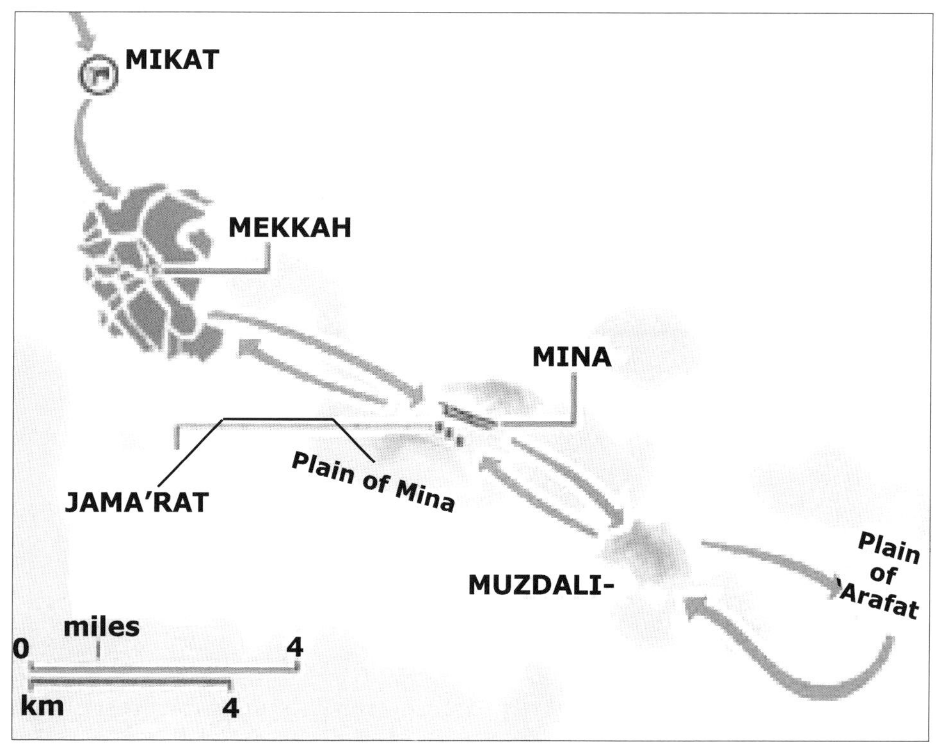

Map of the main Hajj sites

Baqi Cemetery with the Mosque of the Prophet in the background

Wednesday, January 4th

I wake up at 3a.m. because thoughts about people in San Antonio and their requests to pray for them is such a challenge: how do I keep track of them? And how do I perform to the best of my capability? I start to note down the names that I have prayed for so far, but soon determine that I will just take my notebook with me to the *masjid*: it will be easier to keep track of names and that will help me in being fair to everybody.

ALLAH SWT knows best my intention to become the most excellent possible vehicle to deliver *dua* for the various situations, *Insha'Allah*.

In general, my personal feeling about making *salaat* and *dua* is that I *HAVE* been able to better focus; my intent and alertness to be able to express and formulate needs and requests are centered and sincere. My concentration is sustained: constant re-focusing and renewal of meaning for the most effective supplication keeps the mind occupied and sharp, though it's draining.

Still on the bed taking notes, another thought: The week before we left San Antonio, *Hajj* Ali shared with a group at the Muslim Community Center about the four 'steps' of a journey.

The next day I happen to find this same scenario in *Shaykh Fadhlalla-Haeri's* book: 'Journey to Self-Knowledge' <www.nuradeen.com>. *Mulla Sadra* describes four stations or inner unveilings in his variation of the development towards Self-knowledge:

1. Unveiling: From Creation to the Creator
2. Unveiling: With the Creator, by the Courtesy of the Creator
3. Unveiling: From the Creator to Creation, by Permission of the Creator
4. Unveiling: With Creation by Authority of the Creator

I made a copy of the section and have it with me: a constant reminder that an internal process ought to happen on this trip, and maybe these four steps are aids for me to move along. *AllaHuAlim (Allah is He Who Knows Best).*

Madinah is like a religious camp: all needs are taken care of and there's an easy rhythm of going back and forth between spiritual practices and caring for the body.

I am very aware of the attraction of people (first unveiling) in all their various beauties and interesting faces and how this can become a distraction for my eyes and mind. I am grateful that I am aware of this, and looking forward to *Ihram (ritual dress to enter a 'pure' state)* when everyone loses their individuality, and all stand before *ALLAH SWT:* the oneness and equality of all humankind before *Allah SWT*.

This morning, *fajr salaat* was very beautiful: we placed ourselves in the very front, as close as possible to the house of the *Prophet.* We spent an extended time in supplications...I have the notebook with me...and recite *Assma al-Hussna.* The farewell *dua* brings all of us tears, as we have to say good-bye to this contemplative and beautiful visit; goodbyes and salutations to all the *ahlul Bayt* and the *sahaba* that are buried here.

Afternoon: the journey from *Madinah* to *Makkah*

As we leave *Madinah* on the bus, we get a very good view inside the *Baqi* cemetery: it is way bigger than we thought, and there are many stones: are they all designating a place of burial? Do they know who are these *sahaba* and *tabi'in (followers of the sahaba)* buried here? (PS: back home in San Antonio we find out that one of the lady's grandfathers is buried here!)

The ride goes well, traffic wise; checkpoints are congested, but very manageable.

Before we left our hotel, we all did our *ghusl (a greater ablution/purifying shower)* and changed into the clothes for *ihram.*

At the *masjid Shajar'ra (also called masjid Imam-Ali)* we go for *wudhu* (this is one bathing place, unfortunately, where it is nasty, and difficult to come out cleaner that one went in!!!) *Astaghfirul'Lah (may Allah forgive).*

Ladies changed into their clothes for ihram

The *Shaykh* then overhears each person individually as we pronounce our *niyat (intention)* for the state of *ihram*. There's a list of things that disturb this state of purity: we have been reminded again and again, and still it is helpful to read through the list one more time.

Back on the bus, I sit next to *Hajja Khadijah*, whose intention it is to read the complete *Qur'an* during her stay in *Madinah* and once in *Makkah*. I help her finish the last sections of *Qur'an* by reading one *juz*. Then Rika and I commit to read a few *juyuuz* for her during our stay in *Makkah.*

We are a group of ladies, all dressed in brilliant white; the uniformity and pureness brings to my mind, virgins, someone else calls us 'angels'. The men have donned their two pieces of cotton cloth, and they too have now left all put-on individuality; now they are in the state as *ALLAH SWT* created them.

Here starts: *"labaika allahumma labaik; labaika laa sharikala ka labaik; innalhamd, wan ni'mata, laka wal mulk, laa sharikalak."* We pronounce ourselves to be at the service of our Lord:

> "Here I am, oh Allah, here I am.
> Here I am, You have no partners. Here I am.
> Surely all praise and grace and dominion/kingdom is Yours.
> You have no partners."

The men pronounce it forcefully and with lots of gusto; the women's voices are small in comparison: gentle, soothing.

The next bathroom stop, sometime during the dark of the night, between *Madinah* and *Makkah* is a ramshackle roadside place in the middle of the desert, with a cold harsh wind blowing (feels good to me), but the bathroom.... well, yikes! ....Lets not bring that up!!!

The Ka'aba

Thursday, January 5th, *Makkah al-Mukarrama (The Honorable Makkah)*

3:45a.m.: We are driving into *Makkah* at the same time as masses of people from all directions are walking in one flowing stream, to be ready for *fajr salaat*. We have had a change of hotels, and the bus cannot get to this new one, as they have closed the road to allow the pedestrians to move towards the *masjid al-Haram*. (Later in the day we find out that we just passed the Palestine Hotel, which unfortunately will collapse later this morning.) So we walk to our Hotel Munabbawah, a little ways up and through a narrow alley, stepping gingerly between the lines of people set up for prayer in the streets and in front of our hotel.

We take up our rooms and get to nap, while the men of our caravan go ahead to the *Ka'aba* to do the *'umrah tawaf (circumambulation)*. Hajj Ali returns completely drained. The men shower, then rest: the plan is that they accompany the ladies for *tawaf* after they've rested.

While we're waiting, thoughts and feelings of awe focus on where we are and how close we are to The House of God, mentioned in the *Holy Qur'an* as the 'Ancient Sanctuary' re-built by *Prophets Ibrahim and Ishma'el, a.s.*. My prayer is that I can be aware, responsive and deepen into truly FEELING every moment here.

Outside of the Masjid al-Haram

Rika inside the Masjid al-Haram

I brought with me a tiny scrap of paper with notes jotted down from a lesson many years ago. I keep this paper close to me throughout this time, and frequently look at it as a constant reminder. It gives me keywords to focus on and reminds how to learn to enjoy *salaat* and yearn for the sweetness within:

Presence of heart - emptying of *dunya (worldly matters)*; move away from *ghafla (forgetfulness)*

Understanding – the words of *ALLAH;* recite with feeling from the heart

Glorification – with full awareness, at every utterance; reflect on *Asma al-Husna*

Fear with respect – reflect upon *hayiba, khawf, taqwa (various degrees of respect and awe before the Grandeur of Allah SWT)*

Ar-raja' – Hope

Himma: yearning (the heart opens according to what one puts into it)

Shyness and modesty before Almighty Allah – *hiyya*

I am also wanting to be conscious for the second unveiling of the journey according to *Mulla Sadra*: 'with the Creator by the Courtesy of the Creator.' Though these stations make me think that probably I am way out of line here, I still try to understand or find some similitude in my journey of *hajj*.

For now, the reality of opposites is so crass here: for starters, the towering construction sites for future hotel accommodations, contrasted to the poverty of the dilapidated yet inhabited buildings.

We are in the state of *ihram* and awaiting to go for *umrah'*.

Masjid al-Haram and the Ka'aba

Friday, January 6th

I think it is midnight or shortly thereafter, as we make our way, as a group, to the *masjid al-Haram*. The street is bustling with people and businesses, we see the telephone store, where people are waiting in a long line for a chance to call home, and we constantly have to watch our steps so as not to get dirty.

Seeing the *Ka'aba* for the first time, one should have three *dua* ready:

> I pray that Allah SWT keep me on His Path and make my *'ibadah (worship)* strong and meaningful.
>
> I pray that He invites my children to open their minds and hearts towards God awareness.
>
> I pray that *ALLAH SWT* hear all *dua* requests of mine, my family and all praying *Muslims* in San Antonio, and grant better than we ask for.

Our caravan is quite a large group, 101 in total, about 60 ladies. The *Shaykh* again takes the time to listen to each one of our *niyat (intentions)* individually, and even repeats it himself if he thinks our pronunciation is not close enough to *qur'anic Arabic*. So this takes a while. Then, for some reason the group gets split

Rika, Maryam and Narjis outside the Haram

up, and we end up walking back into the pillared section of the *Haram* and sit down, while others go ahead.

This turns out to be a good thing, as it gives us a chance to soak in the atmosphere, look around, pray, read *Qur'an* and help an elderly lady from our caravan.

The *tawaf*: the brothers form a ring around us women, and we begin our circling the *Ka'aba* at the *Hijr Aswad, the black stone.* The *Shaykh* is in the front (or wherever he is), leading and chanting the *dua'* for each *shawt (one circumambulation).*

All I can do is look up at the *Ka'aba,* we are so close...and why is the *kiswa, the cloth*, so dusty and grimy?

I pray that *Allah SWT* accept our *tawaf,* and that the great effort of the men to protect us and provide space for us doesn't 'stain' the purity of our worship: sometimes, the struggle for space is just too tense and harsh on our behalf. It has disturbed other worshippers on the outside of our ring, and especially other ladies, who are in the middle of this sea of humanity, squeezing and getting squeezed. Why should our treatment be different? May *ALLAH SWT* forgive and accept.

Around and around we go, slowly, a bit at a time, with the expected struggle to make it through the bottleneck space between the *Ka'aba* and the *Maqaam (station) Prophet Ibrahim a.s.* My *dua'* during the last few *shawt* are done with good concentration and focus, as I prefer to close my eyes and let myself be pushed along, without having to witness the men's efforts.

Re-enacting s'ay of Hajjar a.s.

Trying to pray the two *rakaat* at the *station of Ibrahim a.s.* is just about impossible, or has to be done very hastily: the whole area behind the *station of Ibrahim* is crowded with people active in worship...and our guardians are urging us on to the next steps: The *sa'y* between *Safa and Marwa*, re-enacting the story of *Hajjar a.s* and remembering our own ceaseless struggle between ego-self, living this worldly existence, and towards complete abandonment into soul-trusting of *ALLAH SWT's* Superior Planning.

Before we get to that area we drink *Zamzam water* and *Hajja* Rika recites the *dua* for us; *Shaykh* Ahmed takes our *niyat for Sa'y.*

Off we go, and immediately I am on my own and am enjoying myself immensely now, moving with the flow, fast walking between the slower people, and running at a quick pace between the designated stretches. At *Safa and at Marwa* I take some time to be sure to reach the designated rocky area before turning back into the flow down the next *sa'y,* seven times back and forth.

It's fun to 'pop' out at *Marwa* and be welcomed by our group (how did they all make it here so fast??) and then there's the *niyat* and the cutting of a small piece of hair. As a happy bunch of white-clad women with the tell-tale orange bandana-scarves we make our way single-filed through the throngs of people now crowding in to the *Ka'aba* for *fajr' salaat,* back to the hotel. That shower, *fajr* and lying down felt so very good; and may *ALLAH SWT* accept our *umrah', Insha'Allah.*

Gold-plated door to the Ka'aba

Saturday, January 7th midnight at the *Ka'aba*

I have lost track of time.

Makkah is the accumulation of *Allah's* greatest diversity-show in all its stark contrasts. The constant 24-hour-long throng of people of *'ibadah*, of commerce, of service and of poverty...it is truly amazing how these narrow streets and small stores absorb it all, and to imagine that it all is ultimately in existence for worship of the Creator.

Hajj Ali asked this question: does love or fear of *ALLAH SWT* drive them to struggle so hard to get to the *hijr al-Aswad*? Are all these millions of people here to be forgiven for their sins? Or does their love for God drive them here?

I think it is perhaps both at the same time.

We are constantly moving back and forth between the hotel and the *Ka'aba*. We stay for extended periods of time, holding our space between the congregational prayers. I have my name list with me and knowingly and with intention am able to pray for all my living family and friends. The ones having passed from this world, our loved ones as well as the ones having passed away during this time of *hajj* are being prayed for after each and every *wajib (obligatory)* prayer in congregation.

We experience worship on all the floors of the *masjid al-Haram*: in front outside the main wall, on level ground with the *Ka'aba,* on the second and third floors. The second floor, I observe has the presence of numerous wheelchair-bound and mentally challenged people: the rent for wheelchairs + a push-boy is quite expensive, and the boys push very fast so as to get this job over with and move on to the next client.

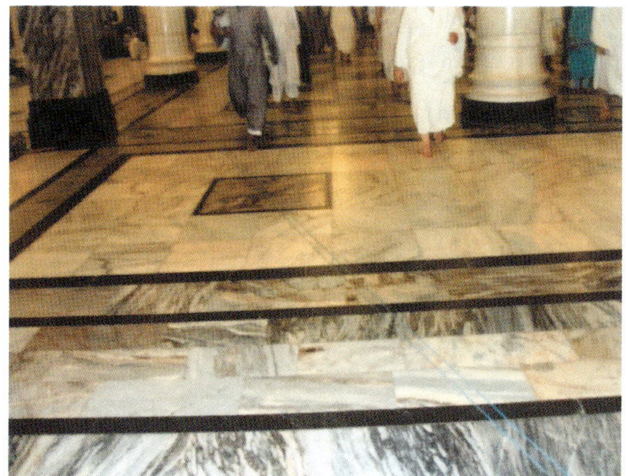

Left: Floor of the Haram. Right: Wheelchair ramp.

I happen to step behind a man who is sitting, and observe how he is following the lines in the *Qur'an* with his finger at an incredible speed: no way can he be 'reading' this: it resembles someone with autism who has found comfort and structure in this activity.

The third floor, the roof, offers its spectacular view of the moving circumambulation around the Ancient Sacred House. That first sight is incredibly dizzying and awesome.

A dead body is carried over the heads and out, a mother has a seizure and falls from her wheelchair, her son sits calmly after securing her head on some towels, feet, hands or elbows bump into various body parts, a bird drops its business down and the cleaning crew needs to clean...humanity in the raw! So many gnarled old people, so many smug young men attached to their cell-phones, and young couples holding hands...it all works by *Allahs' Rahma -Mercy* through time and space.

We drink *Zamzam water* plentifully and nourish ourselves with good meals at the hotel.

Relations with other ladies in the caravan grow slowly. We have the smoking ladies in our rooms' vicinity and this is testing us as is their smoke and smell.

In my *dua'* I am asking *Allah SWT* to guide me in my *ibadah'* and ask for greater precision and understanding.

I ask for deepening of knowledge and correctness of behavior towards others and myself. I ask to become a better and constant servant to *Allah* and to His Creation. I intend to use the time at *fajr* better and more carefully, *Insha'Allah.*

One of the ladies lets me use her cell phone: I briefly talk to Jaffar and Leilah at home and let them know we're ok and I know they're ok. *AlHamdulil'Lah wa Shukrulil'Lah. Hajj* Ali reminds us to focus inward in preparation for *'Arafat*, the great standing before the Almighty.

From *Madinah* to *Makkah*, now on to *'Arafat,* I reflect upon this next step of the journey, the beginning of the *hajj tamattu (the greater hajj)*: the crucial, single pointed focus is on my self, my soul and my Creator. No more masses of people attracting the senses...only *ALLAH SWT* and me. Under the desert stars and in the solitude of a cave is where *Prophets Ibrahim and Muhammad, peace and blessings be upon them*, received their purest states. Is it possible for each of us here to calm the outer vision and turn exclusively to one's inner vision?

"TERROR FOR WORTHLESS REASONS MAY CAUSE DISASTER" and an emergency phone number to call, in case, run in several languages across a neon light banner board at the entrance of the *masjid al-Haram.* (I am surprised at the many, numerous English spelling mistakes everywhere, and here we have a logical mishap: there *never* is a *valuable* reason for terror!)

Makkah has emptied of two-thirds of the *hajjis.* The Saturday night exodus of buses and cars with *hajjis* coming for *umrah'* and leaving to *'Arafat* climaxed in a grand cacophony noise pollution and exhaust fumes. Today, the shopkeepers actually have time to chitchat: we visit Ibn Daoods Superstore (a mall next to the KFC) right in front of the most sacred location in *Islam*!

When we visit the *Haram,* we are actually able to do *tawaf* around the *Ka'aba*, catch a glimpse of the black stone, and are able to look at the stone with *Prophet Ibrahim's* (a.s.) footprints encased in glass. It is time for *'isha*, and quickly the guards shoo us women to the outer circles for *salaat.* Though genders are mixed in this great arena, theoretically there are spaces designated for women and areas preferred by men, and the guards, men and women guards, try to enforce these, with more or less heartiness.

It did catch my attention for a moment at those times, when *Hajj* Ali was praying next to or behind me. Now there's something unusual and different. We walk back to the hotel, and enter into the state of *ihram* again.

Back to the *Haram* to do the *niyat* for *ihram*, then, finally, we are on the bus ride that will take us to *'Arafat*.

Tent City at Arafat

Monday, January 9th, 9th of *Dhul-Hajj* (the month of *Hajj*)

We arrive at the tent city of *'Arafat* in a short and easy ride, maybe around 3a.m. Our tent fills with our women on one side, men on the other; then we try to nap. I am up before *fajr*; the whole morning is so nice and pleasant and *Hajj* Ali takes some time to go over important points and recommended *dua* with us again, which is very appreciated. We also have time to explore these plains a bit, and find we have a nice hill in our 'backyard' to climb later in the afternoon.

Dhuhr and *'asr* are made jointly so as to free the worshipper for the rest of the afternoon until *maghrib*; now the true 'standing' begins and this marks the beginning of the greater *hajj.*

We are actually inside the tent, as there is a visiting *Shaykh* giving some talk in Arabic to the ladies. I remove myself from this stifling and cramped place inside to find a little shade outside the tent.

Inside the men's tent

Almost every tent has started a reading of a *dua* with a loudspeaker: sitting outside I realize there's a lot of noise: the various recitations in different voices and pitch, vigor or gentleness.

*From top: Narjis' "moment";
ladies at prayer;
men at prayer;
Ali dressed up.*

At some point, our *Shaykh* Ahmed is also hooked up to a loudspeaker, and he begins the reading of the *dua* of *Imam Hussein* for the day of *'Arafat*: I brought my copy in English, and follow his Arabic recitation along with my English.

Very quickly, still on the first page, I am suddenly overcome with emotion and overpowered by tears. I mean, I am overwhelmed and awesomely humbled, as thoughts about 'me' flood into my brain. It's not just thoughts, but some physical sensations, too. I can actually feel pressure, strain and ache.

This goes on a while; I keep trying to focus back into the text, but become aware of yet another issue, again and again. By the time our *dua* is over, I am exhausted and drained. I realize there is a silence around me throughout the tents: all recitations have come to an end. It's quiet time, though it's definitely not quiet inside of me. I feel crushed and weighed down.

Through the next hours I am able to sort through thoughts and stuff that had flooded me. It is as if a veil has been lifted somewhere inside and I see clearer now; or as if a trap door in the floor opened and I dropped down to a deep level of truths I had not been aware of:

A consciousness of negative tendencies within me takes on a sharpness and urgency I am not used to. I become thoroughly ashamed of my 'transgressions', or in religious language 'sinfulness'.

ALLAH SWT gives me gifts of self-knowledge today, and like stones they hit me: my weaknesses and sins are such as negligence, arrogance, ignorance, haughtiness, impatience, miserliness, superficiality.

The speed and clarity with which this happens surprises me. Though I am thoroughly ashamed of my 'sinfulness', I am very relieved and grateful to have been shown so clearly and quickly the weapons with which I need to strike *shaytaan* at the *jama'rat.*

The rest of the afternoon I spend off to the side by myself, becoming clearer as to details, trying to formulate the feelings, connecting these to real situations in my life, and then asking forgiveness, giving thanks and praising *ALLAH SWT*. To be in the state of *ihram* and then reflect that I am dressed in my shroud to stand before the Questioning really scares me, when 'sins' are shown this clearly.

Maybe I tasted a bitter/sweet kernel in awesomeness of the second part of the unveiling, 'With the Creator, by Permission of the Creator.' Drained, solemn, as the light slowly changes, the sun will soon be setting. We end this moment of standing at *'Arafat* with the *dua* of *Prophet Adam, a.s*: "Oh Lord, I have transgressed Your Command; I turn to You in repentance, and I seek Your forgiveness" and *maghrib* and *'isha salaat.*

From top: Ladies seeking shade in the heat of the day; Maryam at sunset; gathering pebbles

We board for the short bus ride to *mashad/Muzdalifa*. We pass masses and masses of people walking along the whole stretch. On gravel now we sit outside; it is only that. Darkness. Buses. Noise. Fumes. People. Streetlamps. Nerves. No star studded brilliant night sky, though the crescent moon is straight up ahead and a beautiful, familiar focus once I gingerly lay down.

We are all sitting and waiting for the next step. Leaders of caravans have the 49 pebbles for each individual already collected, and though *Hajj* Ali comes to urge us on to collect the pebbles, I can sense, that if over two million people would have to scoot around looking for pebbles, it would create a terribly dangerous chaos.

Men walking to the stoning of Jama'rat

Tuesday, January 10th, after midnight and into early morning

Skirmishes break out as the exodus begins and people try to catch a ride on buses. There's congestion for the buses to come in to our area, as there's a bottleneck up ahead. We arrive in *Mina* tent city around 4a.m.

We immediately set out for the first stoning of *Jama'rat Aqaba*, the great stone pillar. The walk there is over three miles long; we soon join streams of people, moving through huge tunnels and broad walkways, winding their way along and along.

I am walking along in a bit of agitation, shocked and ashamed of the *shaytaanic* tendencies that have been so clearly shown to me at *'Arafat*. I am still teary, and it only gets worse: depressive thoughts weigh down on me, and my legs feel like lead. I am again and again overcome with sad thinking: here I have been shown the worst side of me, and I do know what to throw the pebbles for, and *Insha'Allah* with this increased awareness, I can better myself (and I cannot wait to prove myself). I look at everyone around me and I wonder what everyone else is going through. All seem so eager to get there, but not me. This is hard.
As I now begin to value the perfection of this whole *hajj* ritual set-up, I become hopeless and deeply depressed: to realize that with millions of people doing this

purification ritual every year, the global impact could be immense. People from the peace movement and their work come to my mind: it seems there ought to be a major shift here each year, with consequences of some worldly dimension, and world peace could become realistic. Haven't we here reached critical mass and a tipping point?

The architectural set-up of the pillar is massive and the crowds manageable at the 'great' *shaytaan*. The intention is said: on each pebble I focus one sin and throw.

This part is easy, piece of cake.

I pray for protection and betterment of myself in each aspect, by and with *Allah's SWT* permission. Not that I actually feel much better. I am confused and still in shock as to all that happened. Someone asks why am I crying? Doesn't every-body feel like crying?

The three miles walk back; everyone is exhausted, and collapses on the mat-tresses to sleep after *fajr.*

The men stayed at *Muzdalifa* until sunrise, then walked to stone the *jama'rat,* then move on to the slaughterhouse for the *sacrifice*; oh, yeah, remember: this is *EID al-Adha.* Each one of us had to individually give permission for the sacrifice to be done in our respective names. We sleep during the day, get fed, stay in the tent.

The news comes that the men have finished the sacrifice; a tiny, insignificant piece of hair gets cut, the men shave their heads.

At *maghrib* we say our *niyat* to stay at *Mina* until the middle of the night, then we will move to *Makkah.*

The slaughterhouse

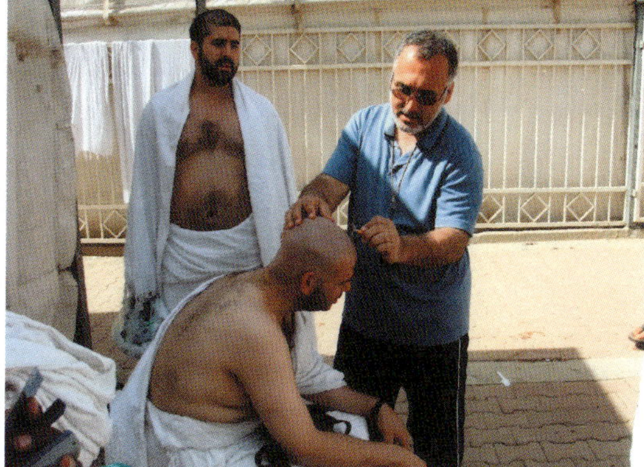

Head shaving

Walking to the stoning

Wednesday, January 11th

At 2 a.m. the bus arrives to drive us to the hotel in *Makkah.* We shower, though stay in a state of *ihram,* and then sleep the couple of hours before *fajr.* The men meantime, went straight to the *Ka'aba* to do their *tawaf* and *sa'y*.

During the night Rika had a serious bout of constriction of her windpipe. We were quite worried; finally she got herself some antibiotic medicine, and fitfully went to sleep.

Breakfast brings us all together, and afterwards everyone gets ready to go back to *Mina.* We approach from a different direction, and move down some wide stairs: we see over the plains and far to the tent cities, and soak in the view of the pedestrian highways with massive streams of people. Again I become very emotional at the sight of this sea of believers . . .

We go down into the pit (or so it seems to me) and begin to stone the small pillar.

My intent on every pebble is formed, the access to each pillar easy.

Something, though, has gripped me and turned my feelings inside out. I am just crying and crying. Maybe it's the great shame about myself, this acknowledgment of my weaknesses, this truth, and all these people doing the same.
I cannot understand the laughing faces...are they happy to have thrown a pebble

Walking through the tunnels to the Jama'rat

at their *shaytaan*? I cry and cry, my knees shake; I am in a crisis, and then I find Rika's shoulder to cry on, and she lets me. The noise and heat is suffocating, and still we are not finished, and there is yet another pillar to strike with my shame. As I gather my determination to settle myself, and get at it again, this becomes my *jihad.* Facing the shamefulness of this all is just so sorrowful.

Though what a therapeutic inner cleansing this turns out to be, and I pray it be so for the many millions that come, and so be able to make space for better, smarter, more patient, compassionate, generous, worshipping persons.

I am soaked and drained at the third pillar; I gather my concentration and focus on each negativity that I want to throw out, or more realistically work on, to be of better service to *Allah SWT*. Climbing back out of the pit, legs still shaking, tears still flowing, I get to breathe again, and am able to gather my feelings and settle myself.

Every time though I turn around to look at this incredible place, I see the masses and it just baffles me, this unbelievable amount of accumulated 'sins' and shames. *ALLAH's* Forgiveness and Mercy on us must be Vast, Infinite and Immeasurable.

We drive back to the hotel, emotions settle, and life seems to return. I do not feel like talking to anyone. Prayers and *Qur'an* reading at the hotel balance me, though tears still well up. I had been praying to *ALLAH SWT*, to open my heart and soften feelings, to feel closer to Him. Maybe this is all an effect of these *dua'*.

This afternoon we will go to the House of God, and that is exactly where I want to go: after facing of my *shayateen*, it almost feels like a coming home to purity, simplicity and safety. Is this to be the third unveiling? 'From the Creator to Creation, by Permission of the Creator'

For the *maghrib salaat* we are back at the *masjid al-Haram* which today is clothed in a brand-new beautiful clean and striking *kiswa*. We continue the next part of our *hajj* ritual: we form up a last time to enter into the circle of people walking around the *Ka'aba*. For some reason, again I find myself exactly in the same spot of the group within the circle. I try to block from my vision and mind, the men holding their arms around our group trying their best to protect us and make the *tawaf* easy; and exactly this effort is distracting me, even unsettling me now. Their efforts are so sincere, though on the outside of our circle, once again, others become greatly disturbed.

In my thoughts, I ask *ALLAH SWT* to remove this responsibility from me, allowing me to put it squarely on the shoulders of our Shaykh (to whom I had spoken about this after the first experience), and to accept my efforts for this *hajj*.

After the *tawaf* we pray our two *rakaat* of thanks at the station of *Ibrahim (a.s.)*: again difficult and disturbed, as the *adhaan* for *maghrib* has been called, and people begin to scamper for space. We move on to the *sa'y*. Throngs of people, much thicker than during *'umrah*, but all goes smoothly and soon we all exit at *Marwa*, our *hajj* almost completed.

I request from *Hajj* Ali to do the *tawaf Nisa* or *Wada* alone; but instead, we four—Hajj Ali and Hajjas Maryam, Rika and I—do this one together on our own, without the group which is forming up again. *Masha'Allah wal Hamdulil'Lah*. It is very jam-packed and congested, but 100% better. There is an empty space just outside the people clinging to the wall of the *Ka'aba*, and we move beautifully through.

We come so close to the *Ka'aba*, but at this particular *tawaf* we are not allowed to touch it. The *kiswa* up close is gorgeous: solid, deep black with the shining gold threaded sewn qur'anic calligraphy. The gold plated door huge up close. We pray at the station of *Ibrahim (a.s.)*, having moved easily out of the circumambulation in the flow of another group with the 'men-around-the-women' formation.

We do not want to leave, and the ease of this *tawaf* has stimulated *Hajj* Ali's yearning to try and touch the wall. Once again we go into the crowd, and let ourselves be moved towards the *Ka'aba*. We are all able to touch the *Yemeni* corner, where it is said, that the wall split open to allow *Fatima bint Asad* to enter, and give birth to the only person born inside the *Ka'aba: Ali ibn Abu Talib a.s.* The crack closed, but is still visible.

We then move on around that corner, and very easily are invited into this empty space where we all place our hands together on the wall of the Sacred Sanctuary, The Ancient House of *Allah*. We pray and give thanks to *ALLAH SWT.*

From the very beginning of this whole journey, *Hajj* Ali and Maryam had intended to renew their marriage vows after completing their *hajj* together. What a magnificent, most perfect moment right now: *Hajj* Ali feels the occasion, and asks Maryam, she confirms, she asks him...he confirms . . . WOW! That was just extraordinarily wonderful, romantic and touching; one of those frozen flashes of light in this moment of eternal time.

Rika kisses the *Ka'aba* and we all rejoice and congratulate Maryam and *Hajj* Ali. We seem to have all the time and space we want, nobody is bothering or pushing us on......But we do move on, life again returns.

We go to the hotel, shower and get ready for another stoning of those darned *shaytaanic* tendencies within me.

We have to return to *Mina* just after midnight, and stay there until dawn. There is bus driver trouble, traffic congestion and time constraints that make this trip difficult.

Up on the roof: Maryam, Rika and Narjis

Thursday, January 12th

Our trip took forever (we didn't arrive until sometime around 3 a.m.) and Rika and another lady whose blood pressure dropped had a very troubled time. As our lengthy bus ride kept turning circles, we passed *'Arafat* and *Muzdalifa* several times, I mean repeatedly, in the darkness of the night, with the eerie yellowish streetlamps lighting up the desert areas strewn with the trash left behind by us millions, and heaps of boxes and trash bags put ready to be picked up. This becomes sort of our 'behind-the-scenes' tour.

Then, at the entrance into the tent city of *Mina*, there's more bus driver trouble: he cannot drive to where he is supposed to take us. Out we file, into the street: we are right in front of the stockyards, where the lucky animals that didn't make it to be sacrificed are standing. There are sheep and camels. This peps Rika up, though she is still having great trouble breathing.

A short wait later, a crumpled old American school bus drives us the rest of the way to our tent. Exhausted we fall asleep.

9 a.m. we get 'breakfast in bed' then off to the *jama'rat*.

Again we walk the three miles. All over again, as the masses gather and march through the tunnels, I see all of us walking towards Judgment Day. This is just fearful, now that I have been given greater knowledge of my lower self, and it is all in my throat, but simultaneously I am extremely grateful to *Allah* that He has gifted me with the right 'munition' to do this with.

Controlling my emotions, and not happy at all, I do the stoning. Each pebble carries its intention and they all hit. Soon we are done ———— that's it! *Hajj* completed!

Mubarak! Mubarak! Victory! Says *Hajj* Ali, though I do not feel that at all: rather the opposite with my conflicting feelings: the tremendous responsibility to return to living with this increased self-awareness of my negativities, but also, knowing now where to better myself, gives great inner peace.

Analyze the fourth unveiling? 'With Creation by Authority of the Creator'. A great challenge from *ALLAH SWT, alHamdulil'Lah wa Shukrulil'Lah.*

Back to the tent, with last views of the masses, masses, coming in for *dhuhr.* (This will be the time then, when sadly the bus accident happens which will make world-news and set everyone at home worrying about us. A passenger bus shed its load of travellers at the access ramps to the Jama'rat Bridge, causing pilgrims to trip, rapidly resulting in a lethal crush. Three hundred and forty six people were killed and many injured.)

We get on our bus, leave *Mina,* and return to *Makkah*. We have finished our fifth obligatory pillar, and everything from now on is relaxation and enjoyment. *Hajja* Rika is still very weak, but *alHamdulil'Lah,* she has been able to do all the obligatory acts, and *Insha'Allah* all of our *hajj* are being accepted.

At the *masjid al-Haram* we join the great congregation for *maghrib*, then go visit the first and second floors. Standing at the third floor railing, and looking down onto the circling, circling, the *tawaf* covering the entire ground floor, and parts of the second and third floor!

We observe the crazed pushing and falling at the corner of the *hijr al-Aswad*, and it looks very, very dangerous and out of control. Up on the roof, we settle in a place towards the back, though not at all out of the way (as if there were such a thing...), and recite *Dua Kumayl* and *Surah Saffat*.

Right as we arrive at the hotel, being very content and peaceful, the ladies tell us to hurry up and get ready for a surprise! *Shaykh* Ahmed is treating everyone to a dinner at a restaurant.

About the food throughout these days: We are very fortunate and grateful to have received the needed nourishment, and the food was safe to eat every time. In the tents, dealing with wastefulness had taken on a pro-active collection to give to the men or the workers, *alHamdulil'Lah.*

A typical meal

This is an observation with a twinkle in the eye: we've consistently been receiving *three* meals a day, which is something I do not do at home, and in addition, I have been served KFC chicken and cola, which I do not get at home. All of it was delicious and lots of socializing fun.

Rika, Narjis, Maryam and Ali sightseeing in the mountains

Friday, January 13th

Today is another historical sites tour day. This is really a tremendous addition to our *caravan*, and proves to be very valuable so as to give the *sirah,* the history of *Prophet Muhammad (saw)* a great deal more relevance.

These are actual true-life mountains and areas, where such-and-such happened.

First stop is at the *Jabal Thaur*. This is where *Prophet (saw)* with *Abu Bakr a.s.* was hiding, fleeing from the *Qureish* who were trying to assassinate him. The cave they were hiding in had a spider spin a web across the opening overnight, and the assassins looked into the cave, but determined that nobody would be in there as this spider had worked a long time to cover the entrance.

Next stop is a return to *'Arafat,* and a close up of *Jabal al-Rahma*, where it is said, that *Prophet Adam* and *Hawa, (Eva)* peace be upon them, came to this worldly existence, after receiving knowledge of discrimination. (There is foodstuff lying around in the sand, but there are no ants. I wonder at this, as ants are mentioned in *Holy Qur'an, Surah 27, al Naml.*)

We visit the *masjid Nemerah* on the plains of *Arafat:* though it is *juma'* day, it is locked up (the clean-up is still in progress); we pray outside the doors and make *dua*. This is where *Prophet Muhammad (saw)* joined the *dhuhr* and *'asr* prayer together for the day of *'Arafat*.

Another stop not far away, brings us to the village at the foot of the *Jabal Noor*; about 5 hours steep climb will bring you up to the cave, where *Prophet Muhammad (saw)* frequently retreated to before his designation as *Prophet and Messenger*: this is where it all began, and the *Angel Jibrail* visited him and gave him the first words of *Surah Iqra (68).* Just standing there and to imagine the *Angel Jibrail* filling all the sky...*subhanal'Lah!* We do not climb it, as this is much more than a short excursion: it is a day trip up and down!

I am imagining young *Muhammad* as an animal herder, roaming these mountainous regions and how he would get to know them so well; I can relate as I got to know so well the details of the forest and surrounding areas of my *Allschwiler Wald* and *DreilaenderEck* of my Swiss homeland; the same way, he would find these caves up in these mountains.

Due to traffic congestion we do not make it as planned to the cemetery of *Abu Muttalib* and his family: he is the grandfather of *Prophet Muhammad (saw).* We return to our hotel in *Makkah*; it is time to prepare for departure: last shopping and packing bags. Rika is staying in bed and staving off a slight fever.

Around 10p.m. we make our last trek through the bustling street, past the vendors in their brightly lit and colorful stalls; past the floor merchants who are mostly women and their children, past bus after bus being loaded up, all idling their motor, and have to dodge the young ones on their motorcycles whizzing by.

Narjis, Rika and Maryam on a final shopping expedition

We have come to say good-bye to the House of God, the Ancient Sanctuary.

Up on the beautiful third floor, we take our time in worship; we praise and thank *ALLAH SWT,* asking Him to protect and guide the young ones; to ease constriction of body and mind for our elders; to open doors to *'ilm*, knowledge and *hikma'*, wisdom, and for best of choices in rulings for our parents and leaders. I ask for constant yearning and learning of proper conduct, *adaab,* for purity of intention and guidance in the *deen* of *Islam* and on the *Siratul-Mustaqim, the Straight Path* for all and everyone.

We complete one *shawt* around the *Ka'aba* on the outskirts of the crowd, pray two *rakaat* behind *Ibrahim's station,* watch the crowds pass under a bridge over the *sa'i,* make *dua* there, then for the very last time up the escalator to the third floor, to the railing to soak in the beautiful circumambulation around the House of God, the One God, Creator and Magnificent, while angels are circling His Throne.

Hajj Ali reads *surah Waqiyah (56)*, and *Hajja* Maryam the translation.

May our children and many of our Brothers and Sisters be able to visit here! May *ALLAH SWT* accept our *hajj,* and invite us to His Presence here sometime again, *Insha'Allah.*

Side Thoughts:

On purification of a whole society:

I want to remember my impressions on watching the change in faces. The faces of women in particular undergo such a tremendous change, as many come into this adventure with make-up on, and the outward façade we all portray is of course not our true self. The state of *'ihram* does not allow putting on any make-up, not even the use of lotion: the purifying effect is quite stunning, as faces naturalize and 'humanize'.

Over the course of the days, faces went from made-up to clean and fresh. The glow after the visit to *masjid Shajar'a* in the new state of *ihram*; the excitement and the thrill at seeing the *masjid al-Haram*; the delight and dignity at *'Arafat* to be in front of the Lord;

The faces then begin to change as weariness sets in at *Muzdalifa.*

It becomes difficult to stave off fatigue and at *Mina* in the dim light of the tent, the faces have so dramatically changed to exhaustion: dark rings around the eyes and no more energy even for a smile. Some sleep revives; the face relaxes and has renewed shine for the next steps.

I found it very beautiful to see this purification of the faces and their entering into a 'real', raw state. (It took but the trip back to London for the make-up to be back on...)

The men's faces change from their initial state not as dramatically as the women's, as they do not have to shed the make-up cover. Though their exhaustion also shows, it is again not as spectacular as the women's. It all also has to do with my eyes' perception, and not being used to seeing women's faces 'in the raw' as much.

Once the men shave their heads, (and so many of them are bald heads!) of course there's a great physical outer change; but there's also the radiance of inner joy and delight with knowledge that *hajj* is almost done.

Walking through the masses in the streets of *Makkah,* I also enjoyed the observation of all the men and women in their clothing; the clothing is attractive and comfortingly blends into a beautiful sea of wholesome colors. There are no T-shirts with all the commercial advertisements or logos or pictures of heroes! No jeans!

What a visual relief! We are not conscious how much the wearing of such 'commercially complemented' garments actually influences our senses and our whole society.

Knowledge of every person being in *wudhu*, the physical washing as well as the intention that goes with *wudhu*, makes this mass of people clean and pure. *Insha'Allah.* There were no bad smells (I noticed in particular the absence of beer smell one gets in American crowds), the only odor being from clothing that became smelly as the person might have had no access to rinse them out.

The ritual of stoning *shaytaan* by millions of people in a condensed moment in time is a most powerful and great tool for purification of humankind on earth.

As we cannot question the intention of each individual, all I can think of, is that humankind, as a whole, has not evolved to a state where it can take true advantage of this tremendous opportunity. Maybe we are too attached to countries' boundaries and nationalities and the many other 'isms.

May *ALLAH SWT* guide leadership around the world, and the generations to come into ego-detachment, just and fair balance, and spiritual wisdom and joy.

Purification of the Self:

Reflecting on the gift *ALLAH SWT* gave me at *'Arafat* and beyond, I remember one fundamental understanding of creation: *ALLAH SWT* created everything in opposites, as an *ayah*, sign pointing towards His Uniqueness and Singularity.

I do not consider myself a sinful person.

In my daily living, my energy is always directed towards bettering myself, being a good person, a serving person, being nice. Preparing to come to *hajj*, I many times asked myself what would be the *shaytaa*n I would throw pebbles at? My sinfulness was the one area that was most obscure and difficult to understand.

Opening up within me deep and real levels of negativities, and the shameful, humbled pain I had to feel, gave me knowledge of spirituality *per se*, encompassing within it both roads, towards goodness and sinfulness. These energies are present: if and how we engage them and in which direction we go, is up to our own individual discrimination and choice.

At once I now receive a better understanding of *dua Kumayl* we read every week and our perpetual astonishment as to how a devout, virtuous true servant of *Allah (SWT)* like *Imam Ali (a.s.)* or *Imam Jaffar as-Sadiq (a.s.)* recognize the need to debase themselves and have such shame. They use such dramatic expressions and with deep sincerity detail their lower tendencies; this always has awed me, and been a spiritual puzzle, to which I now have a little bit of insight, or so I believe.

My asking *Allah's SWT* forgiveness will now take on a new urgency and honest sincerity.

AlHamdulil'Lah wa Shukrulil'Lah

A-Z Glossary

A

Abu Bakr r.a.- he was a life long companion to the *Prophet Muhammed (saw)*; his daughter *Aisha r.a.* was married to the Prophet at a very young age; *Abu Bakr* becomes the first *Khalif* upon the death of the *Prophet.*

'adaab (courteous behavior) – everything is based on *'adaab,* and every moment has its correct and balanced way of behaving, inwardly as well as outwardly; courteous and ethically correct behavior

Adhaan – the call to prayer heard from minarets throughout the Muslim world, alerting the believer to prepare for the next prayer time.

ahlul bayt (people of household) of Prophet – the identity of the *Ahlul Bayt* is to be found in *Qur'an* (ayat-ul Mubahilat 3:60) and *hadith kisa (see H)* and are used by *shi'i* to identify the validity of giving AhlulBayt due credit, which is interpreted differently by some *sunnis.*
For both *sunni* and *shi'i*, love for *AhlBayt* and following the *sunnah* of the *Prophet* are necessary components to be *Muslim*.

Also: *AhlulBayt* – people of the House, describes the family of the *Prophet (saw)* whose lineage reaches down twelve generations, each *Imam* imbued with faultless spiritual and political knowledge; they were always denied leadership and every time martyred, except the last and twelve Imam Mehdi. He was 'taken' to *Allah SWT*, and will stay in hiding (occultation) until the end of time, whence he will return with *Prophet 'Isa* (Jesus) (pbuh) to usher in the reign of peace.

ahlul Suffa (people of the bench) – at the time of the *Prophet (saw)*, a number of especially pious and dedicated individuals perpetually gathered in front of *Prophet's* house on a suffa (possibly from which comes the word: sofa)

Aisha - daughter of *Abu Bakr (r.a.)* and an important *hadith* transmitter in her own right. She was a woman with strong political opinion and not shy about voicing it. In contention with the family of *Ali Ibn AbuTalib,* which will lead to her being a rare woman taking up arms and instigating to battle against him. This is known as the Battle of the Camel. She later repents her initiative into this conflict.

al-Fatihah – first chapter in the Holy Qur'an, translates as 'The Opening' : 1:1-8

AlHamdulil'Lahi Rabbi'l alameen; Praises be to the One, the Lord of the worlds - Frequent, daily expression of re-centering and praising

AlHamdulil"Lah wa Shukrulil'Lah – Praises and Thanks are due to *Allah SWT*

Ali ibn Abu Talib - *Ali* as a young boy is one of the first persons, besides *Khadijah* and *AbuBakr,* to join the *Prophet* as a *Muslim*.
About him the *Prophet (saw)* says, among many other hadith:
"I am the city of knowledge, and Ali is its gate."
"You are to me as Haron (Aaron) is to Prophet Musa (Moses), except that after me there will be no more Prophets.""Of whomever I am maula (master), this, Ali is his maula."

Al-Khandaq (the Battle of the Trench) – the third battle (after *Badr* and *Uhud*), which happened in *Madinah* between the *Muslims* and some jewish tribes. The tactic was new, in that a trench was dug around the place, and the community stayed at the locale, rather than taking the battle outside the town. In this story the 'democratic' character of *Prophet (saw)* is discovered, as he asks for and follows council of other persons.

ALLAH – Al – Lah = The One, besides Whom there is no other

Allahs' Rahmah –*All-Encompassing Mercy* embracing all and everything, unconditionally, as opposed to Ar-Raheem, the Specifically directed Merciful

AllaHuAlim (Allah is He Who Knows Best)- daily, frequent expression

Allschwiler Wald – a forest close to my home in Basel, Switzerland

Angel Jibra'il, Gabriel- the angel designated to transmit messages to the Messengers; same angel for all the Messengers. Other angels have specific functions, such as the 'recording angels', the 'guarding' angels...

a.s. - aleihi salaam – peace be upon him = pbuh: expressing the respect due to persons of Prophecy or holy, spiritually enlightened personalities (saints)

As Salaamu Aleikum wa Rahmatul'Lahi wa barakatu'Hu; Peace be to you, and Mercy and Blessings from Him -
As Salaamu Aleikum – common greeting of peace; in a *hadith*, *Prophet (saw)* says to return a greeting with equal (wa aleikum as Salaam) or better; this expression is 'better' because it asks for more (mercy and blessings) for the recipient.

'asr (late afternoon prayer)- third daily, obligatory ritual prayer.

Asma al-Husna (The Most beautiful Attributes/Names of Allah) –
such as: Ar-Rahman – The Overall Merciful; Ar-Raheem – The Specifically Merciful; Ar Razaaq – The Provider; Ya Wadud – Oh Most Loving; Ya Quddus – Oh Most Holy; Al Zahirun wal Batin – The Manifest and The Hidden; Al Azizul'Hakim – The

Mighty, The Wise, etc.
Ninety-nine *Asma al-Husna* are collected from and used in the *Holy Qur'an*, but His Names and Attributes by necessity have to be unlimited and never-ending.

Astaghfirul'Lah - may Allah forgive - daily, frequent expression

'Arafat – location several miles outside of *Makkah. A Hajji* has to be there at noon on the day of *'Arafat,* and stay in prayer and contemplation until sun-set. It is said, this is the place that *Adam and Hawa (*Eve) *(a.s.)* arrived at, once discrimination and the world of duality was given to them (leaving the paradisical state of bliss).
It is also said, to be the place where *Prophet Ibrahim (a.s.)* was to sacrifice his son.

Ayah – sign; everything created is an ayah, a sign from *Allah SWT* for mankind to reflect upon and remember the Creator;
This is also the name for each verse in the Qur'an: each verse is an ayah, a sign from God, The Wise.

B

Baqi – al Baqi is an attribute of Allah: The Ever-Lasting; Baqi being the name of the cemetery outside the *Prophets masjid.*

Beyrouth – Beirut – I was surprised to see this spelling of the capital city of Lebanon at the airport.

C

Caravan – travel group whose leader acts as the 'protector', especially to women traveling without a male guardian, which is still not permitted in Saudi Arabia; our *caravan* was an American based, majority Lebanese women, youth and men.

D

Deen,(din) -'perfected and all-embracing life-transaction' named *'Islam'* (usually translated as religion)

dhikr (vocal or silent reflection) includes meanings of mention, remembrance, invocation

dhikr beads – a string of beads (various materials and colors; either 33 or 99 beads long plus one more) for purposes of keeping count of the intended number of repetitions in *dhikr.*

DreilaenderEck – german: 'three countries corner' – the exact spot where France, Germany and Switzerland meet together

dua (supplication) – individual prayers, outside the obligatory ritual of *salaat*

Dua Kumayl – a lengthy supplication of Imam *Ali (a.s.),* given upon request to Kumayl, a *shi'a*

dunya (worldly matters) - this world as opposed to the *Aakhira* – the Hereafter – many times *dunya* might be spoken of with a negative connotation: anything that distracts from the awareness to *Allah SWT* is conceived as danger and a challenge. A Muslim is not, however, allowed to completely retreat from involvement with *dunya.* The challenge is to learn not to be controlled by worldly desires, but master the self-discipline of balancing the worldly with the spiritual.

dhuhr salaat (noon prayer) - second daily, obligatory ritual prayer, when the sun has reached its zenith.

E

EID al-Adha – *'eid'* means celebration. For the *Muslim ummah* there are two important world-wide observed *Eid* days: at the end of the fasting-month and on the tenth day of the month of *Hajj*, to commemorate the sacrifice of *Prophet Ibrahim (a.s.).*

F

fajr (early morning) prayer – first daily obligatory ritual prayer before sun-rise

Fatimah bint Asad: 'bint' means daughter of... ('Ibn' means son of...); she is the daughter of Asad, mother of *Ali ibn AbuTalib(a.s.).* She dies soon after childbirth, for which she finds herself inside the Ka'aba. *Prophet Muhammed (saw)* then takes the young Ali into his home and raises him, and marries his daughter, *Fatimah Zahra* to *Ali (a.s.).* It is this special love and relationship of the *Prophet* that makes *Ali* so particularly unique. *Muslim* ladies keep their fathers family name, and do not have to change their name to their husbands.

Fatimah Zahra (a.s.) – beloved daughter of *Prophet Muhammed (saw),* wife to *Ali ibn AbuTalib (a.s.),* mother to *Hasan* and *Hussein, Zaynab* and *UmmKhultum (a.s.);* she is the 'Mother of the Believers' and through her, the lineage of divine guidance is continued through the *'Imams'* up until today.

G

ghafla (forgetfulness) negligence, unaware, opposed to spiritual aware presence

ghusl (a greater ablution/purifying shower) – serves the same purpose (intention to purify) and follows the basic same sequencing as *wudhu*, but involves the whole body (hence as a shower).

H

hadith (a saying/teaching) – a collection of the sayings, examples and practices of the *Prophet.* Besides the *Holy Qur'an* (being the unchallenged Word of *Allah*

SWT) the *Hadith* are the second most important source of knowledge for *Muslims* to actualize the Word of God, following the prophetic example.
There were an uncountable number of collected a*hadith (plural),* and the scientific work to select only the untainted and sound ones was a rigorous and impressive task. There are the two major works of hadith collections accepted in the Muslim world: Sahih Bukhari and Sahih Muslim; there are other and smaller collections, and notably also the *hadith* collection from the storehouse of knowledge of the *AhlulBayt.*

hadith (kisa) – story of the Cloak: ' It was related by UmmSalama (a.s.), that the *Prophet (saw)* covered *Hassan* and *Hussein,* and *Ali* and *Fatimah* with a cloak, then said: "Oh *Allah!* These are the people of my household and my special ones; remove from them impurity, and purify them with a (perfect) purification.' (al Tirmidhi)

Hadith Qudsi – a teaching/inspiration from *Allah SWT* to *Prophet Muhammed (saw)*, but not collected as a revelation in *Qur'an.*

Hajjar (a.s.) – Haggar (pbuh); Egyptian maidservant to Sarah, wife to Prophet Abraham (pbuh); mother of Ishmael (pbuh).

Hajj – fifth of the obligatory five Pillars in Islam: to fulfill the rituals of pilgrimage at *'Arafat to be present, physically and emotionally, at the place of Standing - Muzdalifa, to prepare oneself wth the needed pebbles, inner preparedness for Mina, the place of Stoning ones inner shaytaan – Sacrifice of ones deepest attachment - Ka'aba circumambulating the House of Allah SWT and Sa'y, running the course of total trust in rerceiving 'water', spiritual nourishment* once in ones' lifetime, as long as one has the means and ability to do so.

Hajja Khadijah – everyone is addressed as *'Hajja* or *Hajji;*
Khadijah (a.s.) was the honorable name of the lady who becomes *Prophet Muhammed's* wife of twenty-three years; she broke many social barriers of the existing pagan society as she was a successful business woman, a widow and considerably older than *Muhammed* at the time she proposed marriage to him. She was his greatest supporter and financier on his prophetic mission and is the mother of *Fatimah Zahra (a.s)* (the only surviving child of *Prophet Muhammad's* progeny, through whom his legacy and divine heritage is passed on to *Hassan* and *Hussein* (a.s.). *Khadijah* dies at the end of the *Makkan* period.

hajj tamattu (the greater hajj) – this is the Greater Hajj and is distinguished by its obligation and time sensitivity: if a hajji is not at the place of Standing by noon on the day of 'Arafat, and spends the afternoon there in deep prayer and reflection, then s/he has missed out on that years hajj.

Hamza a.s. – paternal uncle of the *Prophet* and an important support figure; a *sahabi* and strong supporter for the cause of *Islam.*

hayiba, khawf, taqwa (various degrees of respect and awe before the Grandeur of Allah SWT): an intense shaking awe one feels within, when reflecting deeply on the Majesty and Power of Allah.

*Hijr Aswad, the black ston*e – there are varying stories concerning the black corner stone embedded on the *Ka'aba.* We do know, that the *Prophet (saw)* kissed the stone, hence the drive to emulate as close as possible the acknowledgement of the stone.

hikma' – wisdom; *ALLAH SWT* is al-Hakim, the All-Wise; a hakim is the person with knowledge of herbs and medicines and how they affect and interact with conditions of the body, a doctor.

himma - yearning spiritual will; the resolve that overcomes worldly desires, for the purpose of growing closer to God.

hiyya – modesty, shy before the All-Mighty – humble and full of deep respect.

Holy Qur'an – the collection of the revealed words of *Allah SWT*, the Creator and Revealer, to *Prophet Muhammed (saw)* through the *Angel Jibra'il, Gabriel*, over a period of 23 years; as the chosen vehicle of communication *(qur'anic arabic)* from God to mankind, this collection needs to be treated as 'sacred'. Contains 114 chapters of varying length. It is not arranged in order of revelation. Is readily available for anyone to read and study, with appropriate *'adaab,* courtesy.

holy Rawdah – a type of inner sanctuary – a specific small area besides what used to be his home, and now is the gravesite of *Prophet Muhammed (saw)* and his *mimbar*, inside the *masjid.*

I

'ibada (worship) – in its narrow as well as broadest sense, for example, the five obligatory pillars, as well as engaging in humble and aware, God-directed, daily activities.

Ibrahim (a.s.) – Prophet Abraham (pbuh); considered the 'father' of declared 'Monotheism': in *Qur'an,* he is describes as a Submitter - *'muslim'* (though from Prophet Adam (a.s.) until *Prophet Muhammed (saw)* all carried the same teachings to their people): Chapter 2:130-133

> 130:' and who forsakes the religion of Ibrahim but he who makes a fool of himself. And certainly We made him pure in this world and in the Hereafter he is surely among the righteous.
> 131: When his Lord said to him: Submit ('aslim), he said: I submit (aslamtu) myself to the Lord of the worlds.
> 132: And the same did Ibrahim enjoin on his sons, and (so did) Yaqoub (Ja-

cob): 'O my sons, surely Allah has chosen for you (this) religion, so die not unless you are submitting (muslimun) ones.'

Ihram (ritual dress) – women are allowed great freedom in their choice of clothing for *ihram,* but no make up, no lotions, no perfumes; the men must change into two white cotton towels without seams, and wrap them around the upper and lower bodies in a prescribed way. They are not allowed to wear closed shoes, only open sandals. They are not allowed to wear anything on their heads.

'ilm – knowledge; not just academic, rather all-encompassing worldly wise understanding as well as spiritual knowledge.

Imam Jaffar as-Sadiq a.s – He's the great-great-great grandchild of *the Prophet (saw).*

Imam - an *imam* is the one who leads the prayer in particular, and the Muslim community in general.
In *shi'a* tradition, the term *'Imam'* takes on an added meaning: it is the title and function of spiritual authority of *Imam Ali (a.s.)* and his eleven designated descendents.

Insha'Allah – God Willing, if He so Wills it; frequent daily expression.

'isha (late night prayer) - fifth daily, obligatory ritual prayer, in the later evening.

Ishmael (a.s.) – Ismail (pbuh); firstborn son of Abraham (pbuh); Prophet and ancestor to Prophet *Muhammed (saw)*, half-brother to Prophet Ishaq (Isaac) (pbuh), who is ancestor to Prophet "Isa, (Jesus) (pbuh)

Islam
Muslims – salaam- all from the same root: s-l-m – develops into the meaning of 'inwardly' surrendered unto *Allah SWT*, and outwardly professing, with good intention and actions ones convictional belief towards *Allahs SWT's Message* and the *Sunnah* of the *Prophet (saw),* hence (theoretically) leading a life of outer and Inner peace, completely surrendered.

Islam – five obligatory (action) Pillars: 1) shahada (declaration of faith); 2) salaat (5 daily prayers); 3) sawm (fasting); 4) zakat (charity); 5) hajj (pilgrimage to Makkah) –

Iman – Pillars of faith (belief system): 1) Oneness of GOD; 2) belief in Angels and the Unseen; 3) belief in Prophets and messengers; 4) belief in Divine Messages/ Holy Scriptues; 5) belief in the Day of reckoning or Judgement.

Iqamat – (*adhaan* is called first, to let people close shop, turn down the cooking pots, turn off the TV's etc, and wash up for prayer, *wudhu*.)
Iqamat then silences everyone into the prayer lines and directs every individual's attention to the prayer beforehand.

J

Jabal al-Rahma – 'rahma' means mercy = Mount of Mercy to which Adam and Hawa, Eve were brought after expulsion from 'Paradise'

Jabal al-Thaur – the mountain of Thaur – while using a cave on this mountain to hide from pursuing assassins, overnight, a spider webs its weave across the cave mouth. In the morning, as the assassins come to look into the cave, they deduct from the spider-web, that nobody would be inside the cave and leave, saving the lives of *Prophet Muhammed (saw)* and *Abu Bakr (r.a.)*

Jabal Noor – 'noor' (nur) means 'light' - Mountain of Light.

jama'rat – pillar; there are three pillars set apart that one needs to strike with seven pebbles each

jama'rat Aqaba – the great Pillar, symbolizing the great Satan (the most trouble-some to be found within ones self)

Jihad – from 'jahada', meaning, to exert oneself to the outmost, the 'inward' struggle against ones lower, animalistic tendencies; secondary, the struggle against oppression and wrong in society

Juma' – jama' means together; Juma' is Friday, the day of the obligatory (for men only) weekly congregational prayer; women may attend, but are also free to look after their children and home

Juz (plural: juyuuz) – part or parts.
The *Holy Qur'an* consisting of 114 chapters of varying lengths is divided into 30 parts of equal length. It is a worldwide practice to read one *juz* a day during the Fasting-month of *Ramadaan* (third of the obligatory five Pillars in Islam), hence completing a reading of the *Holy Qur'an* in one month.

K

Ka'aba – the cube-shaped building in the heart of *Makkah*;
legend has it that the first foundation was laid by *Prophet Adam (a.s.)*. It was later re-built by *Prophets Ibrahim* and *Ishmael (a.s.)* who established the pilgrimage rites around *the 'Ancient Precinct'.* At the time of *Prophet Muhammed (saw),* the *Ka'aba* was occupied with idol-statues of the many competing tribes, all exhorting 'sacrifices' of wares or monies. At the end of his *Prophethood,* while re-entering and establishing *Makkah* as the most sacred site in *Islam,* he cleaned out all the idols from inside and outside of the *Ka'aba,* renovated it and performed the rituals of the *Hajj* in the form that millions and millions of worshippers have done ever since. There is nothing inside the *Ka'aba.*
The *Ka'aba* is the focus towards which all *Muslims* around the globe face when praying and also when they are buried.

Khalif/Khalifate – vicegerent, representative
In the *Holy Qur'an* the term 'khilafa' describes the high position *Allah SWT* gave

to wo/man on earth: to be His vice-gerent, or representative in creation.
A *Khalif is* the person who is burdened with the political and social leadership of the Muslim *'ummah,* standing in as the representative of *Allah SWT.*
Khilafate was the system adopted after the death of the *Prophet (saw)* and history witnesses four 'righteous' *khulafaah* (plural): (*AbuBakr, Umar ibn al-Khattab, Uthman, and Ali ibn AbuTalib).*
After this period, persons with weakness for power allow corruption, greed and alterior motives to take over leadership of the Muslim *'ummah* and the balanced and just governorship system deviates off the path of Muhammadi Islam.

kiswa, the cloth – every year a new cloth is woven with black thread. Hand-stitched gold plated embroidered verses from the *Holy Qur'an* employ many workers each year. The old cloth will be cut into smaller pieces, and royalties, heads of states, and other dignitaries visiting the *Hajj* will receive a piece for their keeping.

L

"labaika allahumma labaik; labaika laa sharikala ka labaik; innalhamd, wan ni'mata, laka wal mulk, laa sharikalak

> "Here I am, oh Allah, here I am. Here I am, You have no partners. Here I am. Surely all praise and grace and dominion/kingdom is Yours. You have no partners."

In preparation for *hajj* everyone needs to memorize this.

'Le Grande Voyage' (director: Ishmael Faroukhi; a great movie, highly recommended): a father needs to make *hajj,* and has his son drive him from France through Italy, Czechoslovakia, Turkey, down south all the way to *Makkah...*

M

Madinah – in pre-Islam this city was named Yathrib. *Prophet Muhammed (saw)* migrated from *Makkah* to Yathrib (622C.E.), upon which the city's name changed to *Madinah – the city of the Prophet. Madinah* is second most holy place in *Islam* (after *Makkah* and before al-Quds, Jerusalem). Also called Medina.

Madinah al-Munawarra (the city of the Prophet, the Lighted) – discovering another description.

maghrib (prayer after sunset) – fourth daily, obligatory ritual prayer, just after sun-set.

Masaajid – plural of *masjid*; it is questionable to translate *masjid* (sing.) to 'mosque.'

Masha'Allah, God has willed it - daily, frequent expression.

mashad/muzdalifa – station, name of the area, place.

masjid Ali'wa Fatimah – commemorates the location of *Imam Ali (a.s.)* during the battle of the trench. *Shi'a* adoration of anything connected to the *Ahul-Bayt* is a problem for the Wahabi religious authorities, and they have made expressions of love and respect towards the Prophets' Family difficult, in some cases even, illegal.

masjid al-Haram – *haram* means 'sacred', hence the Sacred *Masjid*; includes the *Ka'aba* and all the area around the *Ka'aba*, including the two upper levels, and the area of *Sa'y*. *Masjid al-Haram* is the most sacred place for *Muslims*, so much that non-Muslims are not allowed to enter.

Masjid al-Nubuwiyah or *Masjid al-Nabi (Masjid of the Prophet)* – the place that incorporates the home, the place of worship, and the place of burial of *Prophet Mohammed (saw).*

Also of interest: *Nabi* and *Rasul* :
Allah SWT teaches us to make a distinction between a *Nabi – Prophet*, one who carries the perpetually unchanged divine message to his people of his place and time of which there have been 124'000. In *hadith Qudsi* Allah SWT promises that each and every people/society/nation have had their prophetic voice guiding towards The Creator of all.

And a *Rasul - Messenger* (upon whom revelations by Angel *Jibra'il [Gabriel]* were brought) of which there are four: Prophet/Messenger *Musa (Moses)* with the commandments on the tablets; Prophet/Messenger *Daood (David)* with the *Zabur (Psalms)*; Prophet/Messenger *'Isa (Jesus*) with the *Injil (parts of the Gospel)* and Prophet/Messenger *Muhammed* with the *Qur'an.*

masjid al-Qiblatain. (masjid of two the prayer directions) - *'qibla'* defines the prayer direction

masjid al-Saba (seven-masjid) – lumping the noteworthy individually named *masaajid* together into this one 'new-age' Saudi-style architecture, might diffuse history into ignorance about details of any particular historic events

masjid Shajar'a (also called masjid Imam-Ali)- *shajar'a* means 'tree'. This is one of four 'entry' stations (E, S, W, N) into the area closing in on *Makkah*, offering shower stalls to change into *'ihram*.

Makkah – the spelling 'Mecca' has come to mean any type of congregational attraction, such as 'the Mecca of Motorcycle fans, or the shopping Mecca; *Makkah* being a truer transliteration from Arabic.

Maqaam (station) Prophet Ibrahim (a.s.): contains the rock with an imprint of *Prophet Ibrahims (a.s.)* foot, when *Ishmael (a.s.)* stood on his fathers shoulder to lay more stones up high while re-building the *Ka'aba.*

mimbar (pulpit) – the place designated from which the leader to speaks to the community.

Mina – the extensive tent-city, divided into sections identified by continents.

Mubarak! – Congratulations!

Mulla Sadra : he is also known as Sadr ad-Din ash-Shirazi; a Persian philosopher/ genius who lived from 1571 – 1640 C.E.

N

Narjis Pierre - hajja'amatul'Lah – upon entering *hajj,* every person becomes *hajji* (male) or hajja (female). *Amatul'Lah* is the feminine form of 'Abdul'Lah ; 'abd means 'servant/slave (to The Owner of Everything). Amatul'Lah was another name given to me, besides 'Narjis', upon my taking *shahada*.

niqab-clad (face veiled) – niqab specifically means the face and hand-covering; jilbaab (jalaba), hijaab (hajaba) are other words describing covering or 'curtaining off'...all meant to guide and establish a protected, modest society, which accounts for controlled behavior between men and women. Differences of covering by men and women vary by country, climate and cultures.

niyat (intention) – having a clear formulated and aware purpose for each of the worship practices (*ibadah'*) is almost more important that the ritual itself: what's the use of a ritual if the intention is not clear?

O

Ottoman Khalifate – ruling Muslim power from 1299 – 1922 C.E. comes after a succession of Muslim expansion and political rulership:

Abbasids Dynasty: 750 – 1258 C.E.
Fatimid Dynasty: 909 – 1171 C.E. mostly North Africa & Egypt
Umayyad Dynasty: 661 – 750 C.E.
The four Rightly Guided Khalifate (*AbuBakr, Umar, Uthman, Ali)* 632 – 661 C.E.
Muhammed, The Prophet in Madinah 622 - 632 C.E.

P

Prophet Muhammad (saw) – born around (570 C.E.) in *Makkah*; he is raised first by his grandfather then his uncle as he is orphaned early on in life. Marries wealthy independent business woman *Khadijah;* receives first revelation at age 40 and fulfills the role of 'perfect human being' on the prophetic path until his death at the age of 63, before which the completion of *qur'anic revelations* is achieved and the 'perfection of life-transaction' – *deen* - is named *'Islam'* (*Qur'an 5:3)*

Q

qur'anic revelations/arabic – *Allah SWT* chose arabic as the language of revelation to the Arabs; though the society was imbibed with poetry, the revelations were a whole other dimension of a 'classical' Arabic; the spoken Arabic of pre-Islamic time, and colloquial Arabic spoken today, is crude and simplistic compared to the eloquence, depth and beauty that touches directly into the hearts of even those individuals who do not understand the qur'anic Arabic, but have to rely on the translations given. Translations never impart the powerful strength and sweet fragrance of a true and spiritual understanding.

R

Radhialla anhu- r.a. - may *Allah SWT* be most pleased with him/her.

raja' - hope – never to loose hope of *Allah SWT's* forgiveness, whatever the circumstances may be.

rakaat (prayer cycle) – one cycle of standing, bowing, prostrating to the floor with the accompanying memorized words.

S

sacrifice – this symbolizes the sacrifice of the son that was asked of *Prophet Ibrahim a.s.* We each need to have focus on our greatest worldly love and attachment and be ready to give that up, for *Allah SWT.*

Safa and Marwa: names of the two opposite small hills.

salaat (prayer) – second of the obligatory five Pillars in Islam; a prescribed (in *Qur'an* and *hadith*) set of memorized movements and recitations a certain number of times, directed towards the Ka'aba at certain times of the day and night.

Salman al-Farsi - commemorates the location of Salman al-Farsi (Salman the Persian), a *sahaba,* during the battle of the trench.

sahaba (companions) – followers and companions to the *Prophet Muhammed (saw);* there are varying degrees of closeness: those that sat, walked and learned from the Prophet personally or those that lived during the same time, but never met him; there are those that unconditionally loved and trusted the *Prophet (saw),* and there are those that resisted and argued and questioned.

Sa'y- today a covered air-conditioned walkway between the two hills *Hajjar (a.s.)* ran to and fro between, searching and praying for a solution to her predicament.

Shahada - first of the obligatory five Pillars in *Islam* : a declaration *(shahada=witnessing)* of faith, saying : 'I bear witness that there is only Allah, One God, and I bear witness that Muhammed is Messenger of Allah'.
With this pronunciation in sincerity, one establishes oneself as *'Muslim'.*

shari'a – legal foundation of a society, based upon scriptural commandments.

shawt - one circumambulation of the seven;
for the specialized person or the *Shaykh*, there is a supplication for each *shawt.*

General folks such as myself keep repeating the same *dhikr.*

Shaykh – a learned and wise, (elderly) person*; Shuyuukh (*plural) are teachers, mentors and spiritual guides who have reached a certain degree of enlightenment; today the term is gifted liberally to persons with little more than general islamic knowledge

Shaykh Fadhlalla-Haeri – a truly enlightened, contemporary Shaykh, with many students around the world. I have the distinct honor of being a 'murid' (spiritual student) of his ever since I became *Muslim*, even though our contact has been few and far between. His integrity, clarity and love shine for me every time I read or listen to him: www.nuradeen.com and www.askonline.co.za (Academy of Self-Knowledge)

shaytaan – satan; the verb '*shatana'* means, 'to be far removed from Mercy'

shi'a – the word means 'a follower of...' but has come to identify the followers of *Ali Ibn AbuTalib (a.s.)*
Sunni – comes from the *Sunnah,* which is to exemplify the teachings and way *Prophet (saw)* implemented the revelations.

All Muslims necessarily follow the *Sunnah* of *Prophet Muhammed (saw) and Imam Ali (a.s.),* because he was most knowledgeable and practiced closest to the *Sunnah*, as he lived and walked constantly with the *Prophet (saw).*
The unnatural division into *sunni* and *shi'a* has a political background which began after the death of the *Prophet (saw)*, and is not a religious one.

Sirah – biography of Prophet Muhammed (saw); recommended reading

Siratul-Mustaqim - the Straight Path – from the point of my heart, body, mind and soul to point *ALLAH SWT*; guidance on the *Siratul Mustaqim* is what *Muslims* pray for numerous times in each of the cycles of their daily prayers.

Subhanal'Lah - Glory be to Allah! – daily, frequent expression

surah Ar-Rahman and Al-Waaqi'ah - chapters 55 + 56 - 'The Beneficent' and 'The Event'

Surah al-Fath or Nasr - chapter 110 – The Victory
"In the Name of Allah, the Beneficient, the Merciful

1.When Allah's help and victtoy comes
2.And thou seest men entering the *din* of Allah in companies,
3. Celebrate the praise of thy Lord, and ask His protection. Surely He is ever Returning (to mercy)."

Surah Al-'Alaq - chapter 68 - The Clot - begins with the first word, 'iqra, revealed from *Allah SWT* and transmitted by *Angel Ji'brail* to *Prophet Mohammed (saw). Iqra* means 'recite' or 'read' (*qur'an* means 'recitation):

"In the Name of Allah, the Beneficient, the Merciful

1. Read in the name of thy Lord who creates –
2. Creates man from a clot
3. Read and thy Lord is most Generous
4. Who taught by the pen
5. Taught man what he knew not."

Surah Saffat – chapter 37 – 'The Ranks'

surah Ma'ida - chapter 5: The Table spread or The Food, verse 6

(saw, pbuh – sallalahu aleihi wa sallem – peace and blessings be unto him) – expression after mentioning the name of *Prophet Muhammed (saw)*

SWT – Subhana wa ta'Ala – Glorified be He, the Highest

T

tabi'in (followers of the sahaba) – the companions (*sahaba)* of the Prophet each in their individual right became a teacher and specialist; their students are the *tabi'in*, and the students of these are the *tabi'in of the tabi'in*.

tahhajud (superogatory night prayer) – in the dark of the night, alone in worship to the One, a different set of prayer-cycles

tawaf (circumambulation) – *tawaf* consists of a set of seven circuits around the *Ka'aba*, beginning at the corner of the 'Black Stone'.

Tawaf Nisa or Wada – Nisa – woman / wada – farewell circumambulation: this is the last circling of the Ka'aba in the *hajj* ritual, and allows one to come out of the state of *ihram*

The movie: 'The Message' – The Story of Islam – 1998 - Director: Moustapha Akkad with Anthony Quinn, Irene Papas. The movie is a good piece of work detailing the story of Prophet with relative accuracy. Recommended.

U

Uhud – second important historic battle in the year 625 C.E. just on the outskirts of *Madinah,* between the Muslims and the tribe of Qur'eish, the dominating ruling party from *Makkah,*

Umar r.a.- was initially resistant, even hostile to the *Prophet* and the young *Muslim* community; he resented his sister becoming *muslim*, and wanted to punish her for it; as he approached her home though, he heard *Qur'anic recitation*, and in one instant his heart got touched, and opened up into a life-long passion for *Prophet Muhammed* (saw) and the Message of Islam; his daughter Sawda was married to the *Prophet*; *Umar (r.a.)* is elected to the second *Kalif* after *Abu Bakr r.a.*

'umrah – follows a similar set of rituals (circumambulation, *sa'y* and cutting of hair) excepting the standing at *'Arafat,* the night at *Muzdalifa* and the stoning at *Mina*. 'Umrah can be done at any time of the year and is not time-sensitive as is *hajj*. *'Umrah* does not replace *hajj.*

umma' (community) – includes the whole Muslim society with all aspects, locally, and as a world-community, as a distinct and integrated community.

V

various madhaab – school of thought – come into existence some time after the death of *Prophet Muhammed (saw)* around figureheads of leadership in interpretation of *shar'ia* – Imam Jajjar al-Sadiq, Imam Malik, Imam Hanifa, Imam Hanbali, Imam Sha'fi – the five dominant schools of legal interpretation.

W

wajib (obligatory) – it is a sin not to fulfill what *Allah SWT* ordered to be an obligation

wudhu' (ablution) - a rinsing of the mouth and nose, a wiping of the face, arms, top of the head, and feet following a learned procedure; necessary to prepare for prayer.

wudhu and tayamumm (ablution) – *wudhu* is the cleansing ritual before prayer; if there is no water available, then the alternative is *tayamumm*, which follows the same procedure but with dust or dirt.

Y

Yemeni corner: each corner has its own name and significance: the southern corner will be pointing to Yemen.

Z

Zamzam water – the well that miraculously appeared and saved the lives of *Hajjar* and *Prophet Ishmael (a.s.)* and which has flowed ever since and still today harbors scientific wonders, such as its good taste, its richness in minerals, its quality and its never-ending flow, quenching the thirst of millions of visitors.

NARJIS PIERRE

My mother, a British nurse, accompanied her friend on a working trip to Australia; my father, a Swiss typographer, accepted a job in Australia. On a weekend visit to the Island of Tasmania, they on the ferry, fell in love, and soon married.

I was born in 1957 in Melbourne, Australia. I was potty-trained on the long ship voyage back to Europe, detoured by way of South Africa because the Suez Canal was blocked, up to Paris and then on to settle in Basel, Switzerland.

Three younger brothers followed to complete the family; we all started out as English-speakers, but quickly switched to 'Swiss' as we successively entered kindergarten. My mother mostly retained English spoken at home.

Our upbringing did not include a structured religious identification, though Mother definitely had deep faith and love for her church, whereas Dad didn't really mind any. Living right next to a church, and with mandatory religion classes in public school, he probably thought that would give us enough religious guidance.

I entered work force at age 18 with a pre-practicum, working in an institutional home for children and young adults with cerebral palsy. The next three years were spent at pedagogical school, which included a practicum at the home & school for 'Shippers' children (off the barges on the Rhine) and the last practicum at the 'Stationary Psychiatric Department of the Children's hospital', where I stayed on after graduation to work for another three years.

In the early 80s I became involved in the political scene. Environmental challenges, proposed nuclear sites and their unresolved issue of waste discharge, luxury renovations and a overall 'police state' atmosphere heightened by several terrorist incidents around Europe jolted all of us into an ideological debate of whether physical force was necessary, or peaceful methods such as sit-ins and boycotts had enough power to effect change.

Various combinations of communal living situations gave me plenty of opportunities to live and practice conflict resolution, justice and generosity, and forced us to widen all of our horizons.

The restless young mind is quick to criticize, and that we did plenty, and in the course of time I became quite involved in the democratic process. Then disillusionment set in and the time came to search for that better life elsewhere. Friends traveled to far and wonderful places: to Turkey and into North and Central African countries. Possible volunteer opportunities in Nicaragua made me choose to travel to South and Central America.

For one half year I traveled by bus from Lima, Peru up north through Ecuador, south of Colombia, to San Andres Island and Guatemala. There I met an American family and together by train we traveled to the border at Laredo, and then around the southern part of Texas, until I decided to honor an invitation to stay at a rural Muslim community outside Blanco, Texas.

Here, before long, I had to make a most important decision: to continue traveling the world or return to Switzerland. But there opened before me an unexpected alternative: I could embark on a quest for knowledge of God and the purpose of existence, to which the Muslim ladies joyously were challenging and inviting me.

So, I stayed and said *shahada,* metaphorically agreeing to believe that all the beauty of nature was a creation by intelligence – a God – and that I had never heard of a Prophet named Mohammed and knew nothing about him, did not bother me.

A couple months later, I married, and this is what truly made the roots dig deep and firm into the ground of Texas. We raised three children living frugal and healthy in the country and partly home schooling our children. American city life took over when our family moved into San Antonio and the culture of TV and 'fitting in' became dominant.

I became involved in the local Muslim community, co-founding SAMWA (San Antonio Muslim Women's Association), staying pretty stable and committed. Presence in Tri-Faith Dialogue of San Antonio and an invitation to serve on the Board of the peaceCENTER expanded my connections into the non-Muslim communities, and my service there has always helped me to learn more and grow on the Path towards Peace and Light, in a nice balance together with the Islamic/Sufi teachings of Shaykh Fadhlalla-Haeri, my inspiration and guide.

Made in the USA